LEEDS CASTLE

Maidstone, Kent ME17 1PL England

Tel +44 (0) 1622 765400   Fax +44 (0) 1622 735616

email   enquiries@leeds-castle.co.uk
www.leeds-castle.com

Coat of arms of Catherine de Valois, widow of King Henry V, over the Queen's Room fireplace.

Written and designed by Nick McCann.

Photography mainly by Peter Smith
of Newbery Smith Photography.

Other photographers include:
Phil Dent, Barry Duffield, Angelo Hornak, David Hoskins, David Markson,
Edmund Nägele, David Noble, Chris Parker, Derek Shuff,
Skyscan Balloon Photography front cover, Andy Williams and Tony Zirkel.

The publishers are grateful to the following for their contributions to the
text and content: David Cleggett, Historian, Paul Sabin, Chief Executive,
Andrew Wells, Curator.

Project managed by the Leeds Castle Marketing and Business
Development Department.

Leeds Castle Foundation is grateful to the following:

Mr RF Robertson-Glasgow for the loan of paintings:
Archbishop Robinson (Chapel Corridor, page 18), Edward VI,
Brueghel/Keil painting (Queen's Gallery, page 28), de Heem still life
(Queen's Gallery, page 28, pages 91/92).

The Church Wardens and Parochial Church Council of St Michael and all
Angels, Withyham, East Sussex, for the loan of the Gerini paintings in the
Chapel (page 36).

The Lynne Wilson Trust for the loan of the bookcase in the Boardroom.

Produced and published for
Leeds Castle Enterprises Ltd.
by Heritage House Group Ltd.
Heritage House, Lodge Lane, Derby DE1 3HE
Tel +44 (0)1332 347087   Fax +44 (0)1332 290688
email   publications@hhgroup.co.uk
www.hhgroup.co.uk

Printed in Great Britain

Disabled visitors are especially welcome. Full details of accessibility and special facilities
throughout the castle and grounds are listed in a leaflet available on request either in
advance or on arrival. We regret no dogs can be admitted except for guide dogs or
hearing dogs.

Changes may be made to works of art, furniture and other items on display in the Castle
or elsewhere on the Leeds Castle Estate. Parts of the Castle and other facilities may be
closed from time to time without notice.

"Wonderful in manifold glories are the great castle visions of Europe; Windsor from the Thames, Warwick or Ludlow from their riversides, Conway or Caernarvon from the sea, Amboise from the Loire, Aigues Mortes from the lagoons, Carcassonne, Coucy, Falaise and Château Gaillard – beautiful as they are and crowned with praise, are not comparable in beauty as with Leeds, beheld among the waters on an autumnal evening when the bracken is golden and there is a faint blue mist among the trees – the loveliest castle, as thus beheld, in the whole world."

LORD CONWAY

"THE LOVELIEST CASTLE IN THE WORLD"

CONTENTS

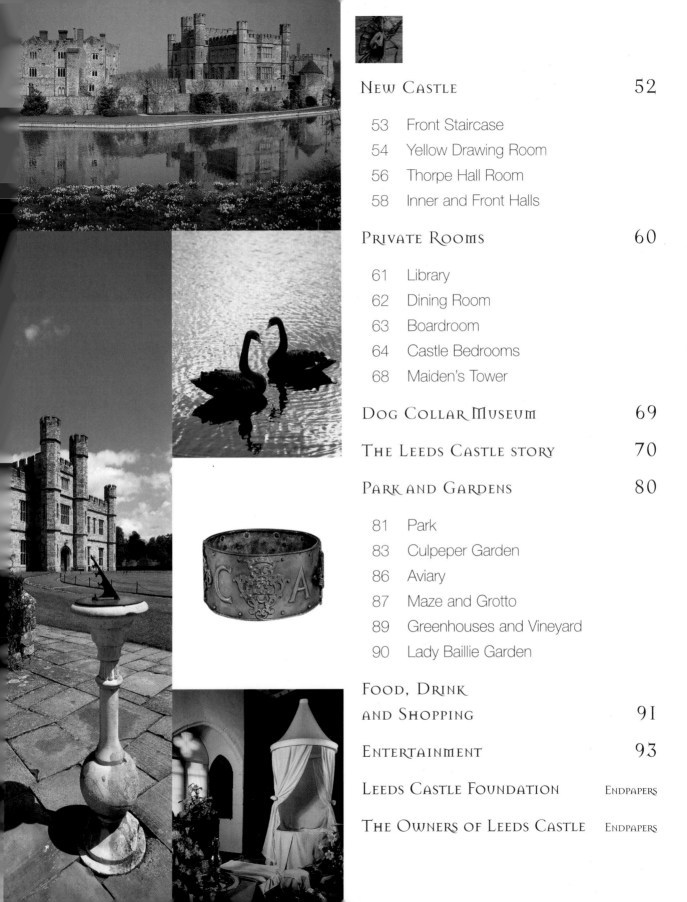

INTRODUCTION

LEEDS CASTLE

A CASTLE FOR ALL SEASONS AND ONE OF THE MOST ROMANTIC AND HISTORIC BUILDINGS IN THE LAND.

Listed in Domesday Book, this castle has been a Norman stronghold, a royal residence for six of England's medieval queens, a palace of Henry VIII, and a retreat for the powerful and influential.

The castle was raised in stone on an island by a Norman baron in the reign of William the Conqueror's son, Henry I, nearly 900 years ago. 150 years later it came into the possession of Edward I, the founder of our Parliament, and for the next three centuries it remained a royal home. It later passed into the hands of three famous families, the St Legers, the Culpepers and the Fairfaxes, and was owned for just over a century by the Wykeham Martins, until it was bought in 1926 by the Hon Mrs Wilson Filmer (later the Hon Olive, Lady Baillie), a wealthy Anglo-American heiress. The castle was her lifelong love, and, with great vision and considerable generosity she ensured that after her death the castle, managed by the Leeds Castle Foundation, would be enjoyed by visitors from all over the world.

The Foundation's objectives are to preserve the castle and park in perpetuity for the benefit and enjoyment of the public; to enable use of the castle for important national and international meetings, particularly for the advancement of medical research and for the furtherance of peace; and to promote artistic events. Leeds Castle receives no major grants or government funding, and therefore the income raised from visitors, conferences, private functions, the golf course and special events, including open-air concerts, is essential for the continued preservation of this unique heritage site for future generations. Leeds is preserved as a living castle, and now visitors of all nationalities, interests and ages can spend a full day enjoying the many attractions of the castle, gardens and park.

Opposite:

THE BLACK SWAN;
a symbol of Leeds Castle.

MAP AND GUIDE to LEEDS CASTLE and GARDENS

1   Main Entrance
2   Ticket Office
3   Park Shop, Plant Centre and Privilege Pass Desk
4   Car Park
5   Disabled Car Park
6   Coach Park
7   Duckery
8   Cedar Pond
9   Wood Garden
10   Pavilion and Garden
11   Barbican and Fortified Mill
12   Gate House, Dog Collar Museum and Shop
13   New Castle

← To Maidstone and M20 J8

B2163

A20

A20

Golf Centre and shop

Golf Course

Golf Course

Cedar Lawn

Main Drive

Moat

Visitor Route

Upper Car Park

Map by Nick McCann

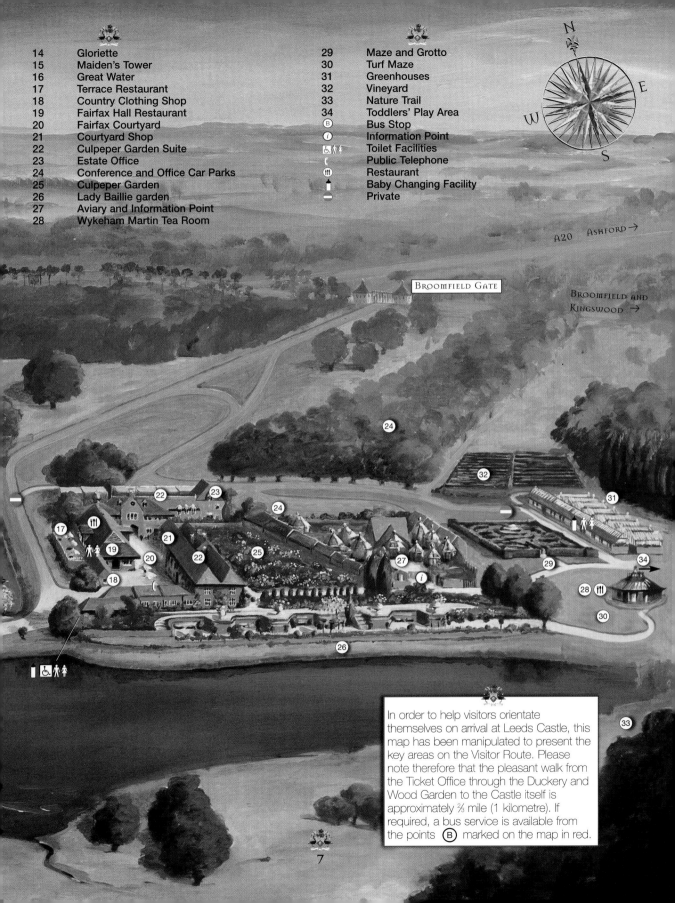

14 Gloriette
15 Maiden's Tower
16 Great Water
17 Terrace Restaurant
18 Country Clothing Shop
19 Fairfax Hall Restaurant
20 Fairfax Courtyard
21 Courtyard Shop
22 Culpeper Garden Suite
23 Estate Office
24 Conference and Office Car Parks
25 Culpeper Garden
26 Lady Baillie garden
27 Aviary and Information Point
28 Wykeham Martin Tea Room

29 Maze and Grotto
30 Turf Maze
31 Greenhouses
32 Vineyard
33 Nature Trail
34 Toddlers' Play Area
Ⓑ Bus Stop
ⓘ Information Point
Toilet Facilities
Public Telephone
Restaurant
Baby Changing Facility
Private

A20 ASHFORD →

BROOMFIELD GATE

BROOMFIELD AND KINGSWOOD →

In order to help visitors orientate themselves on arrival at Leeds Castle, this map has been manipulated to present the key areas on the Visitor Route. Please note therefore that the pleasant walk from the Ticket Office through the Duckery and Wood Garden to the Castle itself is approximately ⅔ mile (1 kilometre). If required, a bus service is available from the points Ⓑ marked on the map in red.

LEEDS CASTLE'S ARCHITECTURE

KEEP OR 'GLORIETTE'

13th century

BRIDGE CORRIDORS

rebuilt 19th century

NEW CASTLE

rebuilt 19th century

details from a PANORAMA showing the west prospect of the castle, taken from an estate map drawn by Thomas Hogben in 1748.

Courtesy of the Centre for Kentish Studies, Kent County Council

HAS DEVELOPED OVER NINE CENTURIES

MAIDEN'S TOWER

late Tudor

REVETMENT WALL

c. 1280

GATEHOUSE

13th century   late Norman

TOUR OF THE CASTLE

SUNK WITHIN THE FOUNDATIONS OF THE NORMAN BUILDING,

the cellar is the oldest surviving visible part of the castle's interior and originally may have been a convenient means of entry, or swift escape route via the moat outside.

CELLAR AND STAIRS

Its shallow pointed vault dates from the late 12th century and runs the whole depth of the building. In the right hand wall, an intriguing archway, the only rounded Norman example in the castle, leads through to a blocked-up stone staircase, which gave access to the medieval great hall above. It is believed that more cellars existed, but minor investigations have revealed nothing yet. The cellar is dry and cool and for centuries has been used for the storage of alcohol, as recorded in inventories taken at the deaths of 2nd Lord Culpeper (1689) and Catherine, Lady Fairfax (1719). The southern part of the cellar is used for the secure storage of wine for conferences and banquets held at the castle.

THE ESTATE'S OWN WINE, *which is displayed near the staircase, is made from grapes grown in the same part of the estate as the vineyard recorded at Leeds in Domesday Book in 1086.*

At the top of the stairs is a display of weapons and the funeral hatchment showing the coat of arms of Fiennes Wykeham Martin, who rebuilt the New Castle in 1822.

In the vault on the half-landing is a complete suit of
EUROPEAN CUIRASSIER ARMOUR
dating from the early 17th century.

This type of suit, consisting of close helmet, cuirass (breastplate and backplate), and long tassets for protecting the thighs, was used by heavy cavalry soldiers.

Heraldry Room

Descent of Leeds Castle 1552–1926

(names in capitals indicate ownership)

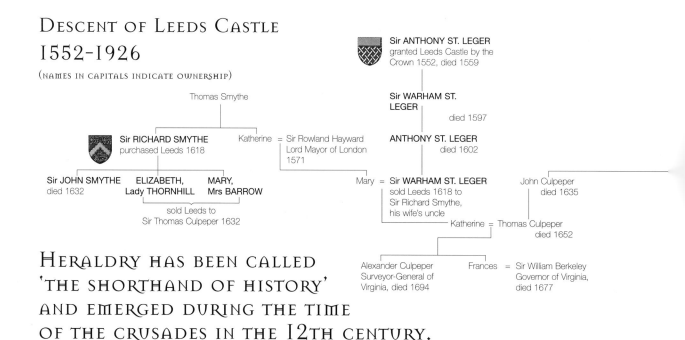

Thomas Smythe

Sir RICHARD SMYTHE
purchased Leeds 1618

Katherine = Sir Rowland Hayward
Lord Mayor of London
1571

Sir JOHN SMYTHE
died 1632

ELIZABETH,
Lady THORNHILL

MARY,
Mrs BARROW

sold Leeds to
Sir Thomas Culpeper 1632

Sir ANTHONY ST. LEGER
granted Leeds Castle by the
Crown 1552, died 1559

Sir WARHAM ST.
LEGER
died 1597

ANTHONY ST. LEGER
died 1602

Mary = Sir WARHAM ST. LEGER
sold Leeds 1618 to
Sir Richard Smythe,
his wife's uncle

John Culpeper
died 1635

Katherine = Thomas Culpeper
died 1652

Alexander Culpeper
Surveyor-General of
Virginia, died 1694

Frances = Sir William Berkeley
Governor of Virginia,
died 1677

Heraldry has been called 'the shorthand of history' and emerged during the time of the crusades in the 12th century.

It was a graphic system to distinguish one family or individual from another, especially useful in the confusion of battle or tournaments, or during complex occasions of state and the ceremonial of marriages and funerals. Experts in the creation of such signs and symbols became known as heralds. In the room hang portraits of several distinguished members of the Fairfax family which owned Leeds Castle through most of the 18th century. The 3rd lord, "Black Tom", the great Civil War parliamentary general, is portrayed twice. Also on view is his buff coat, worn at the Battle of Maidstone, where he defeated the royal army in 1648.

As its name suggests, the room displays the coats of arms of the private owners of Leeds together with those sovereigns associated with the castle. The Kings of Arms granted a coat of arms to Leeds Castle Foundation in 1999 to mark its 25th anniversary.

In 1552, after almost 300 years of royal ownership, the castle became the seat of several inter-connected families. It descended through these by blood or purchase for the next four centuries, until acquired by the Hon Mrs Wilson Filmer (later Lady Baillie) in 1926.

Originally the site of the great hall of the medieval castle, the room was redesigned as a library in 1927 by Lady Baillie's architect, Owen Little.

Jacobean strapwork ceiling
cast from moulds taken from originals at the Victoria and Albert Museum, from Sir Peter Pindar's house in Bishopsgate, London c.1620.

| Sir Thomas Fairfax of Denton | 1st Lord Fairfax | 2nd Lord Fairfax | 3rd Lord Fairfax | 5th Lord Fairfax |

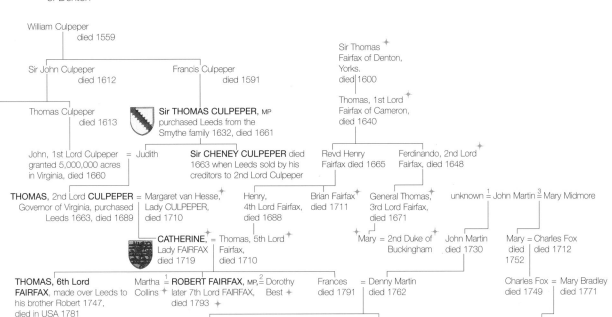

William Culpeper died 1559

Sir John Culpeper died 1612

Francis Culpeper died 1591

Sir Thomas Fairfax of Denton, Yorks. died 1600

Thomas, 1st Lord Fairfax of Cameron, died 1640

Thomas Culpeper died 1613

Sir THOMAS CULPEPER, MP purchased Leeds from the Smythe family 1632, died 1661

John, 1st Lord Culpeper granted 5,000,000 acres in Virginia, died 1660 = Judith

Sir CHENEY CULPEPER died 1663 when Leeds sold by his creditors to 2nd Lord Culpeper

Revd Henry Fairfax died 1665

Ferdinando, 2nd Lord Fairfax, died 1648

THOMAS, 2nd Lord CULPEPER, Governor of Virginia, purchased Leeds 1663, died 1689 = Margaret van Hesse, Lady CULPEPER, died 1710

Henry, 4th Lord Fairfax, died 1688

Brian Fairfax, died 1711

General Thomas, 3rd Lord Fairfax, died 1671

unknown $\overset{1}{=}$ John Martin $\overset{3}{=}$ Mary Midmore

CATHERINE, Lady FAIRFAX, died 1719 = Thomas, 5th Lord Fairfax, died 1710

Mary = 2nd Duke of Buckingham

John Martin died 1730

Mary died 1752 = Charles Fox died 1712

THOMAS, 6th Lord FAIRFAX, made over Leeds to his brother Robert 1747, died in USA 1781

Martha Collins $\overset{1}{=}$ ROBERT FAIRFAX, MP, $\overset{2}{=}$ Dorothy Best later 7th Lord FAIRFAX, died 1793

Frances died 1791 = Denny Martin died 1762

Charles Fox died 1749 = Mary Bradley died 1771

Revd DENNY MARTIN, took name of FAIRFAX 1782, died 1800

General PHILIP MARTIN, died 1821, leaving Leeds to kinsman Fiennes Wykeham

Revd Richard Wykeham died 1805 = Mary died 1808

Eliza Bignell died 1863 = FIENNES WYKEHAM, took name of WYKEHAM MARTIN 1821 on inheriting Leeds from General Philip Martin, died 1840

 Portrait at Leeds Castle

Lady Jemima Mann, daughter of $\overset{1}{=}$ CHARLES WYKEHAM MARTIN, MP $\overset{2}{=}$ Matilda Trollope
5th Earl Cornwallis, died 1836 | died 1870 | died 1871

Elizabeth Ward died 1893 = PHILIP WYKEHAM MARTIN, MP died 1878

Fiennes Wykeham Martin took name of Cornwallis 1859, died 1867 = Harriet Mott died 1884

Cornwallis Wykeham Martin died 1903 = Anne Rolls died 1912

CORNWALLIS PHILIP WYKEHAM MARTIN, died 1924 = Anne Draffen died 1923

Fiennes, 1st Lord Cornwallis (2nd creation)

Glenrose Goodall died 1928 $\overset{1}{=}$ FAIRFAX WYKEHAM MARTIN, died 1952 (sold Leeds to Hon Mrs Wilson Filmer (later Hon Lady BAILLIE) 1926) $\overset{2}{=}$ Ann Hutton

Fiennes Fairfax Wykeham Martin, died 1984 bequeathing many family portraits and chattels to the Leeds Castle Foundation

Right: ROBERT, 7TH LORD FAIRFAX (1706-93) *and the Fairfax arms. Fairfax was an officer in the Life Guards when this portrait was painted by John Vanderbank c.1730. He later commanded the West Kent Militia and became MP for Maidstone and then Kent.*

Drawing of Leeds Castle from the north by Eliza Wykeham Martin 1822.

Drawing of the Gloriette from the north by William Twopeny 1822.

LOWER BRIDGE

CORRIDOR

THE PRESENT BRIDGE

linking the New Castle to the Gloriette is a remarkable structure, containing the two corridors on the visitor route, and a third above these.

Weapons and armour spanning several centuries guide the way to the Gloriette, an area where the changes made by Lady Baillie and the Foundation have aimed to give the castle an appearance which might have been familiar to its occupants in the 15th and 16th centuries.

This portrait of
HENRIETTA MARIA (1609-69) AFTER VAN DYCK
hangs at the north end of the corridor.

The Queen of Charles I and daughter of Henry IV of France, she was accompanied during her exile in Paris by the Royalist 1st Lord Culpeper (father of the 2nd lord who purchased Leeds Castle from the trustees of his parliamentarian cousin, Sir Cheney Culpeper).

GLORIETTE

A Spanish term for a pavilion at the intersection of a Moorish garden ~ arising from ELEANOR OF CASTILE'S influence.

The complete internal restoration of the Gloriette was commissioned by Lady Baillie and supervised by ARMAND ALBERT RATEAU (*1882-1938*), *a Parisian architect and interior designer of considerable repute. He rebuilt the interior, installing oak floors, ceiling beams and doors, and the Fountain Court half-timbering. He designed many other features such as the spiral staircase, the screen of stone arches and several iron light fittings.*

Carved mythical beast on the Gloriette stairs

Half-timbering of the south wall of the Fountain Court

Detail of a 16th century CARVED OAK PANEL *containing royal portraits and heraldic shields.*

Mary, Duchess of Buckingham, only child of 3rd Lord Fairfax c. 1660.

George Villiers, 2nd Duke of Buckingham 1662.

CHAPEL CORRIDOR

BEAUTIFULLY CARVED FURNITURE AND PANELLING

characterise this corridor.

On the early 17th century carved and inlaid oak press cupboard is a bronze bust of a boy thought to be Louis XIV of France, *c.* 1640. Above it hangs a portrait of the Most Reverend Richard Robinson (1709-94), Archbishop of Armagh, by one of England's greatest artists, the flamboyant first president of the Royal Academy, Sir Joshua Reynolds. The frame is surmounted by a carved gilt mitre. At each end of the corridor hangs early 17th century pikeman's armour.

Sir Edmund Cary c. 1650, father-in-law of Brian Fairfax, uncle of 5th lord.

Q
U
E
E
N'
S

R
O
O
M
S

QUEEN'S ROOM

CATHERINE DE VALOIS WAS A 21 YEAR OLD FRENCH PRINCESS WHEN HER HUSBAND KING HENRY V OF ENGLAND DIED.

She soon fell in love with Owen Tudor, the Welsh Clerk of her Wardrobe, but when the couple's romance was discovered, they were both imprisoned. The queen was later released and Tudor escaped from prison. They secretly married, and their son Edmund became the father of Henry VII and thus began England's remarkable Tudor dynasty.

THE ARMS
of Queen Catherine, incorporating the three lions of England and the three fleurs-de-lys of France. The use of a lozenge, rather than a shield, signifies that she was a widow.

A STATE BED OF EXAGGERATED SIZE, SYMBOLISING THE QUEEN'S LOFTY STATUS,

*By permission of The British Library
French manuscript Harl. MS4431*

Following Lady Baillie's reconstruction of the Gloriette's historic interiors, the Leeds Castle Foundation felt it appropriate to create in this room and the Queen's Bathroom the luxurious surroundings which royal ladies might have enjoyed in the 15th century. In 1984 the room was redesigned, based on evidence from contemporary sources such as the significant French illuminated manuscript (*left*), which shows Queen Catherine's mother, Isabel of Bavaria, receiving a book of her poems from Christine de Pisan. The damask wall hangings and bed draperies incorporate the monogram HC (Henry and Catherine) entwined with a lover's knot, signifying the union and desired peace between England and France through the marriage of King Henry and Catherine de Valois in 1420.

IS EQUIPPED WITH A CANOPY OF EQUAL SIZE, AND IS RAISED ON A SMALL DAIS.

QUEEN OF CASTLES

SYMBOLISM WAS IMPORTANT

in furniture and decoration. The raised state chair and golden crown surmounting the canopy of the day-bed ensured a prominent position for the queen. This is not a bedroom so much as a grand chamber where the queen conducted much of her business, receiving advisers, courtiers and petitioners; its sumptuousness guaranteed that her visitors could only be awestruck.

THE BED
has three curtains to provide a complete screen when required, with the front curtain often looped up during the daytime. The framework is entirely of oak.

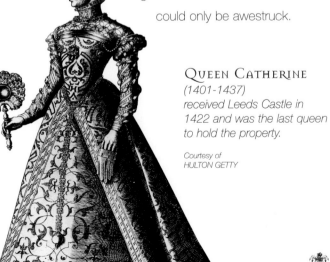

QUEEN CATHERINE
*(1401-1437)
received Leeds Castle in 1422 and was the last queen to hold the property.*

*Courtesy of
HULTON GETTY*

HENRY V
*(1387-1422)
on the occasion of his Coronation 21st March 1413.*

*Courtesy of
HULTON GETTY*

CASTLE OF QUEENS

Queen's Bathroom

Etiquette and courtly customs

were as important here as anywhere else in the castle, and here again the walls are hung with damask.

The tub, albeit a surprisingly humble structure beneath its hangings, is surrounded by a fine white circular curtain which hangs from a sparver canopy, again denoting rank, suspended from the ceiling. Like the state bed, these furnishings were designed to be easily dismantled when the queen was not in residence and the valuable hangings would have been moved to her next abode or stored.

The bath would have been filled with herb-scented water and emptied through the tap fitted in its base.

Engraving of
QUEEN CATHERINE
DE VALOIS
'from a curious limning in a prayer book'.

Courtesy of Private Collection /
Bridgeman Art Library

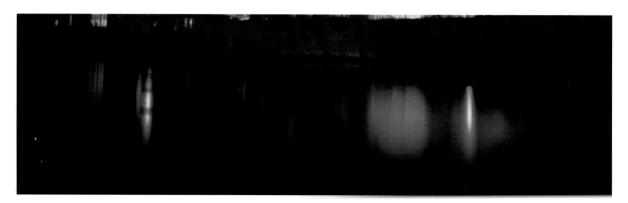

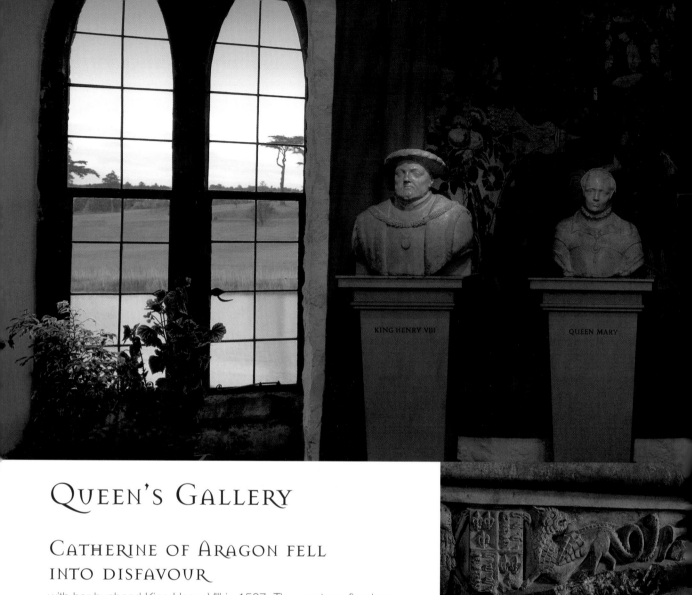

Queen's Gallery

Catherine of Aragon fell into disfavour

with her husband King Henry VIII in 1527. The ragstone fireplace must have been part of his refurbishments at Leeds before this date, because the left spandrel (*above right*) contains the arms of the House of Lancaster, from which the Tudors descended, and the Tudor dragon with a serpent added to its tail, while the right spandrel (*right*) contains the castle of Castile and pomegranates of Aragon. Originally in the queen's withdrawing room (now Lady Baillie's bedroom), the fireplace was installed in the gallery by Lady Baillie's designer, Rateau, in the late 1920s at the same time as the ornate beams, carved with designs of grapes and serpents by French and Italian craftsmen.

QUEEN ELIZABETH I

KING EDWARD VI

The impressive iron fireback (*left*), was made in 1997 by Lord Charteris of Amisfield (1913-99), a trustee of Leeds Castle Foundation and former Private Secretary to HM The Queen. It features an heraldic shield with the arms of Edward I and Eleanor of Castile, surrounded by a parrot, a toucan and a cockatoo. The pointed windows date from the 13th century and in 1414 an inventory described the room as "the second chamber". Over the years it has been used variously as an assembly room and a kitchen. Four handsome marble busts of King Henry VIII and his three children who ascended the throne, Edward VI, Mary I and Elizabeth I, recall the Tudor dynasty which was so important to Leeds. They are thought to have been carved by an English sculptor before 1569, and were commissioned by John, 7th Lord Lumley, and depict the four monarchs through whose reigns he lived. As a backdrop to the clean white Italian marble, the mid-16th century Flemish verdure tapestry is rich in colourful foliage, flowers, birds and fruit.

KING EDWARD VI (reigned 1547-1553)

was the only son of Henry VIII and his third Queen, Jane Seymour. He was celebrated as a linguist, scholar and was a strict Protestant. In his portrait above the fireplace (left), he can be seen holding a bible, and his misshapen ear is clearly shown, differing from many other portraits of him. The king wears the collar of the Order of the Garter, composed of red roses, in contrast to the red and white Tudor roses of Henry VIII. Garter collars have had red roses ever since. The picture was painted by or after the Netherlander Gwillim Scrots or Stretes, shortly before the king died of consumption in 1553. The elaborately carved frame, however, dates from the early-18th century.

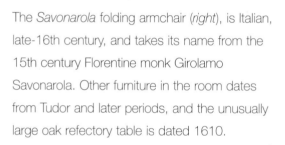

The *Savonarola* folding armchair (*right*), is Italian, late-16th century, and takes its name from the 15th century Florentine monk Girolamo Savonarola. Other furniture in the room dates from Tudor and later periods, and the unusually large oak refectory table is dated 1610.

All the elements of a sumptuous banquet, oysters, a lobster, grapes and strawberries, are shown in the picture (detail *below left*), attributed to a Dutch artist who worked in England, Jan Janszoon de Heem (*b*. 1650).

In the picture of a young girl, with a monkey and fruit in a landscape (detail *left*), by Abraham Brueghel (1631-90) and Bernhard Keil (1624-87), it has been discovered by recent X-ray research that the girl was painted by Keil over the smaller figure of a baby. Brueghel, the great-grandson of Pieter Bruegel the elder, was responsible for the remainder of the picture. In the third quarter of the 17th century both men lived in the same street in Rome.

Opposite:

THE FOUNTAIN COURT,

showing Lady Baillie's paternal arms (of Paget) flying from the turret.

FOUNTAIN COURT

WATER IS SUPPLIED TO THE CASTLE

today from the same springs in the park that fed cisterns underneath the courtyard in the 14th century.

This part of the castle, the central courtyard of the Gloriette, dates from the 1280s, but as these pictures (*right*), show, not everything is what it seems.

Left: A carved dragon decorates the oak jetty beam.

Drawing of the courtyard with lath and plaster walls prior to the present stone walls of 1822.

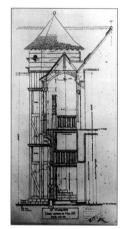

Rateau's plans for the screen and tower containing the spiral staircase.

Work in progress in 1929.

Opposite: Leeds Castle was a palace of HENRY VIII. *Between 1517 and 1523, Sir Henry Guildford undertook extensive restoration and enlargement of the buildings for the king. This portrait by an unknown English artist hangs in the Henry VIII Banqueting Hall.*

Originally a larger courtyard, the 7th Lord Fairfax built lath and plaster walls which were replaced with the present stone walls in 1822. However, the most remarkable transformation took place in the late 1920s, when Lady Baillie's decorator and architect Rateau built the timber-framed '16th century' screen incorporating the spiral staircase. The lead downpipes were embellished with Tudor roses, scallop shells and wildfowl. The Italianate marble fountain was supplied by a local Maidstone mason in the late-19th century. The remarkable skill of Rateau and his craftsmen created a feature of Leeds Castle which is memorable for its beauty as well as its apparent historical authenticity.

HENRY VIII

Henry VIII Banqueting Hall

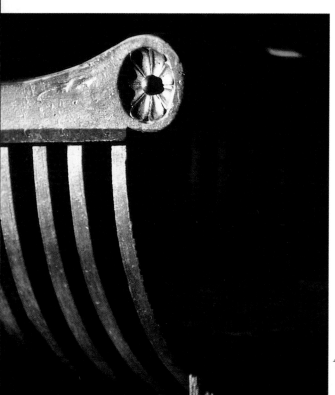

Left: Detail of 16th century Italian Savonarola armchair.

The rare early iron fireback dates from Edward IV's reign (1461-83) and features the crowned royal arms with three fleurs-de-lys, supported on the left by a lion and on the right, a leopard.

Measuring 73 feet

from one end to the other, this is the largest room in the castle. It still gives some illusion of dating from the time of Henry VIII when the bay window was built, although the structural features were completely altered for Lady Baillie. Rateau installed the superb carved beams of the ceiling and the magnificent ebony floor with its double-dovetailed joints, which is believed to be unique; his most important addition was the French 16th century carved Caen stone fireplace, with its figures, lions and Bacchus-inspired grotesque heads, brought from a château in the Ile de France.

The Banqueting Hall contains some important paintings, furniture and sculpture, and the earliest known Enghien tapestry retaining the town's and its weaver's marks. Dating from between 1513 and 1535, this rare armorial tapestry commemorates Anthoine de Jauche-Mastaing, Baillie of Enghien (*d*.1535). In its centre a palisade encloses a helmeted lion bearing the Jauche arms.

Spring scene by Pieter Brueghel the younger (1564-1637/8).

ebony floor   Enghien armorial tapestry   carved fireplace: Bacchus   carved oak beam

Embarkation from Dover of Henry VIII

opposite:

On 20th May 1520 Henry VIII set off from Greenwich with an entourage of 3,997 people for his meeting on 7th June with King Francis I of France at the Field of the Cloth of Gold. Henry and his entourage stayed at Leeds Castle on 22nd May, en route for Dover where they embarked on 31st May.

Henry VIII can be seen amidships on the vessel with the yellow sails second from right. The painting was probably executed a generation after the event. Individual ships have not been identified, but they may represent the best of Henry's fleet, not necessarily the actual ships in which they sailed in 1520. The considerable attention to detail, and the ceaseless activity and motion of the painting, suggest the work of several hands. Flemish influence is particularly evident in the figures in the foreground, many of whom would have lodged at Leeds.

St. Barbara
patron saint of artillery, holds a tower in her left hand, recalling the tower in which she was imprisoned to discourage suitors. When she became a Christian, her father, Dioscorus, beheaded her and was immediately struck by lightning.

This 14th century Burgundian limestone figure shows traces of polychrome colouring, a common feature of medieval sculpture. It stands on a Venetian stone pedestal comprising four octagonal columns.

Venetian marble roundel
of carved birds c.1300 of Byzantine influence.

The intriguing portrait of members of the Tudor and Stuart royal families, considered unique in the composition of its subject matter if a little primitive in execution, is thought to have been commissioned by King James I of England and VI of Scotland (middle right), or his Stuart descendants, to prove his claim to the English throne. It emphasizes his descent from the Tudors, through his great-great-grandfather Henry VII, and his dynastic links with the continent through his wife Anne of Denmark (below him) and his son-in-law Frederick, King of Bohemia (bottom left).

The double portrait, dated 1598, by Robert Peake, Serjeant-Painter to James I, shows Mary Penestone and her son Thomas, who was created a baronet in 1612. Her family, the Somers, lived near Rochester, and by her second husband, Sir Alexander Temple, MP, she was the great-grandmother of the celebrated Sarah Churchill, wife of the 1st Duke of Marlborough.

The double portrait of King Richard II and Ralph, 1st Lord Lumley is one of a series of idealised portraits of his ancestors painted before 1590 for the 7th Lord Lumley and attributed to Sir William Segar. It marks the year the first lord was summoned to Parliament 1384, and shows the King holding a document (presumably Lumley's writ), in his right hand, not the orb he holds in his famous contemporary portrait in Westminster Abbey (copied at the north end of the Banqueting Hall). More Lumley portraits hang in the Dog Collar Museum.

The handsome portrait of the unidentified lady in a silvery white dress is one of several from Lady Baillie's collection attributed to Marcus Gheeraerts the younger (1561-1635).

Christ washing the disciple's feet

Judas betraying Christ with a kiss

The flagellation of Christ

The mocking of Christ

Details from four paintings of
THE PASSION OF CHRIST
by Niccolò di Pietro Gerini (d.1415).

A leading 14th century Florentine artist, Gerini's surviving frescoes may be seen in the Church of Santa Croce in Florence. The paintings at Leeds, in egg tempera, were produced sometime between 1390 and 1400. They are remarkable, not least that they are among the earliest surviving paintings on canvas and are striking for their feeling of depth, perspective, space and action.

CHAPEL

RECONSECRATED BY THE ARCHBISHOP OF CANTERBURY in 1978, the

Chapel is used for occasional services. Its history may be traced back to Edward I, when he established a chantry in 1293 for masses to be celebrated to commemorate his first queen, Eleanor of Castile. Since then there have been several changes of use and structural alterations. The room contains many pieces of interest, including a late-18th century mahogany chamber organ, with gilded lime carvings and ebony inlay, believed to have been owned by the Rt Hon Spencer Perceval (1762-1812), the only British Prime Minister to have been assassinated.

Four early-16th century South German limewood carved panels. Possibly originating from Ülm, they retain most of their original paint and gilding, remarkable for their richness.

| THE ANNUNCIATION | THE NATIVITY | THE ADORATION | THE CIRCUMCISION AND PRESENTATION OF CHRIST |

Above the altar hangs a late-15th century Flemish tapestry depicting the Adoration of the Magi, probably woven in Tournai. It once belonged to Lady Baillie's second husband, Mr Arthur Wilson Filmer, a considerable collector himself.

Flemish 14th century
GILT COPPER MORSE,
a large ornamental buckle
joining the two sides of a
cope on the wearer's chest,
showing St Matthew
surrounded by four
apostles in roundels.

**COMMUNION CUP
AND PATEN,**
Robert Smythier,
London 1664.

COMMUNION PLATE,
by Robert Smythier,
London 1664 or 1677.

This silver is loaned to Leeds Castle by the Church Wardens and Parochial Church Council of Holy Trinity Church, Queenborough, Kent, to which it was presented by Sir Joseph Williamson, Secretary of State to King Charles II and founder of the Mathematical School at Rochester, endowed on his death in 1701.

Carved oak
MYTHICAL BEAST

SPIRAL STAIRCASE
and GLORIETTE LANDING

A LAUGHING CRUSADER,

complete with sword, shield and lion cub, is the centrepiece of Rateau's 16th century-style staircase built in 1929. The newel post on which it stands was carved from a single tree trunk. The walls are lined with oak linenfold panelling, which contains several carved mythical beasts and birds.

The clock on the landing facing the stairs was built by William Downie of Edinburgh *c.*1770. This type of clock was common in coaching inns where timekeeping was essential, hence the name 'tavern clock'. After 1797 they became known as 'Act of Parliament' clocks, following a tax being imposed on all timepieces, and private clocks and watches were often hidden or sold to avoid tax. Beneath the clock is an English oak chest *c.*1670.

The carved oak
LAUGHING CRUSADER
holds an equally enigmatic shield, showing a grinning lion sticking his tongue out, the customary heraldic portrayal.

Through the archway from the landing, the walls are hung with pen and wash drawings by

CONSTANTIN GUYS (1802-92).

An untrained artist, Guys used his talents to illustrate his dispatches during his career as a war correspondent, covering the European Revolutions in 1848 and the Crimean War in 1854. In 1824, as a young man of 22, he fought in the Greek War of Independence where Lord Byron, the poet, also served. Although Guys died in poverty in Paris, his work is now highly valued.

These lively spirited pictures of Paris's fashionable *demi-monde* were part of Lady Baillie's collection.

BOARDROOM CORRIDOR

Following major damage caused by Dutch and French prisoners of war in the 1660s, the rooms off this passage were roofless and unusable until rebuilt by the Wykeham Martins in 1822-23. They incorporated several oak doorcases decorated with royal badges dating from Henry VIII's reconstruction.

Off the corridor is the Boardroom, which can be viewed when not in use for conferences, and is illustrated on page 61.

One of Lady Baillie's many and varied interests was her love of birds, in art and in nature. In every room in the castle there are ornaments in the form of birds and several of the corridors are hung with paintings, watercolours, prints and drawings of birds. The first aviaries at the castle were established in the 1950s to house her growing collection of rare and exotic species.

In this corridor hang several watercolours (upper level) of birds in Lady Baillie's aviary in 1970-72, painted by Philip Rickman (1891-1982), 'the Grand Old Man of British Bird Painting'. In addition there are several early-19th century coloured engravings of birds by John Gould FRS, the leading ornithologist of his day, and William Hart (above).

SEMINAR ROOM

16th century North Italian oak figure of St. George and the Dragon, sculpted under Leonardo da Vinci's influence.

Lady Baillie's taste was eclectic, and she collected what appealed to her. Although many of her great Impressionist paintings have been dispersed, this room retains some important pictures.

Watercolour of a French mill by André Dunoyer de Segonzac (1884-1974).

Beach scene, one of three paintings by Maurice Brianchon (1899-1979).

A portrait of Olive Paget (later Lady Baillie), aged about two c.1901, hangs to the left of the fireplace. The portrait of her younger sister, Dorothy, aged about three c.1908, is on its right.

SEMINAR ROOM

In 1978 Mr Mohammed Ibrahim Karmel, General Moshe Dayan, and Mr Cyrus Vance, the Foreign Ministers of Egypt, Israel and the United States of America respectively, gathered around a circular table in this room for the initial talks which culminated in the signing of the Camp David Agreement. Leeds Castle thenceforth became a significant conference centre with an international reputation, and this room took its name from those momentous beginnings.

The room is now designed to take the residue of Lady Baillie's collection of Impressionist paintings. The Wykeham Martins reconstructed it in 1822-23, turning it into a billiard room and reversing the damage done in the 1660s by prisoners of war. Lady Baillie used it at first as her boudoir, her designer, Rateau, installing theatrically gilded mouldings and panelling. Only his chimneypiece and radiator covers remain.

The two red ministerial boxes were used by Lord Geoffrey-Lloyd, first Chairman of the Leeds Castle Foundation, when he was Parliamentary Private Secretary (1935) to the Rt Hon Stanley Baldwin, Prime Minister at that time.

As the only known painting from life of Lady Baillie, this picture is of great importance to Leeds Castle.

Lady Baillie
and her daughters

In 1948 Lady Baillie commissioned a friend and protégé of the Duke and Duchess of Windsor, the French artist, Etienne Drian (1885-1961), to produce this conversation piece of herself and her two young married daughters, Susan (*above left*) and Pauline (*above right*), pictured in the bay window of the Thorpe Hall Room (*here*).

Drian's preliminary sketches of Lady Baillie's daughters, Susan Russell (above left), and Pauline Ward (left), hang in the Catherine of Aragon bedroom, formerly Lady Baillie's boudoir.

Lady Baillie's

Rooms

CORRIDOR

Opposite: Lady Baillie's Dressing Room and Bathroom.

DECORATED WITH BIRDS OF GREAT VARIETY,

this corridor leads to rooms used by Lady Baillie: a dressing room with its adjoining bathroom, her bedroom, and her former boudoir, now called the Catherine of Aragon Bedroom.

Among many pictures of birds are a series of French 18th century watercolours, including the purple heron and great crested grebe, and coloured lithographs of birds such as the bird of paradise.

purple heron   birds of paradise   great crested grebe

A dress and a coat worn by Lady Baillie (Olive Paget), when a young girl.

DRESSING ROOM and BATHROOM

CREATED BY ARMAND ALBERT RATEAU

in 1928-29, these opulent rooms are light and feminine and reminiscent of the style of Louis XVI, although in many ways are unmistakably late 1920s. They epitomise the requirements of Lady Baillie, a leading hostess of that era.

The sumptuous bathroom can be glimpsed from the dressing room. Walls lined with brown Russian onyx, specially made towels incorporating the Leeds Castle black swans, and luxurious fixtures and fittings all give a tantalising hint of her lifestyle in the second quarter of the 20th century.

BEDROOM

BLUE PANELLING

dominates this room designed by Stéphane Boudin, who first
visited Leeds in January 1936. He conceived it as a French
bedroom in the *Régence* style of the early 18th century,
installing *boiserie* (panelling) with several doors concealed in
it. The soaring white half-tester bed, also designed by him,
accentuates the height and depth of the panelling, which
was wire-brushed to raise the grain, limed, glazed and finally
beeswaxed to create the effect of the period.

Several pieces of beautiful 18th century furniture add to the
overall atmosphere. These include Italian lacquer bedside
tables, an ornate French table with a rare Italian scagliola top
decorated with scrolls and flowers dated 1748, and an
elegant gilt-bronze mounted black and red lacquer
commode, Louis XV c.1760.

*Lady Baillie's love of birds is evident throughout her
rooms. On the walls of the bedroom are three pairs of
famille rose cranes of the Qianlong period (1736-95).
A pair of small famille rose hawks, dating from the 19th
century, flank the mantelpiece clock (above).*

Used as Queen Catherine of Aragon's bedroom after Henry VIII's improvements to the Gloriette, this room was General Philip Martin's bedroom in the early-19th century, and in the 20th Sir Adrian Baillie's. Boudin's last commission for Lady Baillie was to convert it to her boudoir in the 1960s, when he hung the present striking hand-locked wallpaper.
It is regretted that this room may not be on view when in use for conferences.

CATHERINE OF ARAGON BEDROOM

Over the bed hangs a portrait of Lady Baillie's mother, Mrs Almeric Paget (formerly Pauline Whitney), by Mark Milbanke. Above the fireplace is a portrait by Jules Laure of Lola Montez, mistress of the composer Liszt and King Ludwig I of Bavaria, whose abdication she caused in 1848. Drian's sketches of her daughters for Lady Baillie's conversation piece in the Seminar Room are displayed on the south wall.

Water-colour of scene near Honfleur by Johan Barthold Jongkind (1819-91).

Upper Bridge Corridor

Leaving the gothic atmosphere

of the Gloriette, the corridor, lit by windows on both sides, seems unusually bright. The north end of the corridor is flanked by drawings of Lady Baillie's terrier *Smudge* and her great danes *Boots* and *Danny* by Alejo Vidal-Quadras, a fashionable Spanish artist, in 1971. Further along the corridor are portraits of *Golden Miller* (1939) and *Insurance* (1934) owned by Lady Baillie's sister, Miss Dorothy Paget, and painted by Thomas P Earl. The legendary *Golden Miller* won the Cheltenham Gold Cup five times and in 1934 won the Grand National as well as the Gold Cup.

Dorothy Paget (1905-60) was an energetic, if eccentric, woman with a range of philanthropic and sporting interests. In the 1930s she stabled some of her horses in what is now the Fairfax Yard, their loosebox doors painted in her blue and gold racing colours – some of her racing silks are displayed in the Fairfax Restaurant bar. She enjoyed sponsoring Bentley racing and backed the celebrated racing driver, Sir Henry Birkin, Bt. She also founded a hospital in Paris for émigré Russian officers.

Boots and Danny

Broad tail whydah by Hayes

White stork by Hayes

Lining the middle of the corridor are water-colour drawings of exotic birds by William Hayes, a leading English ornithologist and bird artist, mainly dating from the 1780s, while at the south end are three gouache and water-colour bird paintings by Peter Paillou *c.*1790, a Frenchman working in London.

Golden Miller

Female marsh harrier by Paillou

The NEW CASTLE

The external appearance of the New Castle has remained largely unaltered since it was rebuilt in 1822.

Front Staircase

THE HON. CATHERINE CULPEPER (c.1670-1719)

This portrait of the heiress of Leeds (c.1673), can be seen over the top flight of stairs in a fine Sunderland frame. Only child of the 2nd Lord Culpeper, and later the wife of the 5th Lord Fairfax, she has at her feet a King Charles spaniel, a symbol of the Culpeper's attachment to the House of Stuart. The picture cannot be attributed with certainty, but a likely artist is Adrian Hanneman.

Lady Baillie installed this carved marble coat of arms of the Duke of Segorbe and Cardona, head of the Aragon family. A Knight of the Golden Fleece, he died in 1670.

The Flemish equestrian tapestries were commissioned by William Cavendish, 1st Duke of Newcastle (1593-1677) from Michael Wauters, based on Abraham van Diepenbeke's illustrations for the Duke's book on horsemanship published in 1658. In the bottom tapestry King Charles II is mounted in front of London before the fire of 1666, while the duke and his page are shown above the half landing. The other two depict Captain Mazin, the duke's riding master, with Welbeck Abbey, the duke's Nottinghamshire seat, in the lower one.

King Charles II - detail of tapestry above the lower flight of stairs.

FRONT STAIRCASE

TAPESTRIES AND PICTURES

are the main features of the Landing and Front Staircase, which was rebuilt for Lady Baillie by Boudin in the 1950s. Her earlier decorator and architect Rateau had inserted the French Gothic-style beamed ceiling, in a similar fashion to those in the Gloriette, in the late 1920s. Either side of the central screen are a pair of 16th century-style neo-gothic torchères which support pricket candlesticks, and above the arches are three English cavalry breastplates and a sword dating from the mid-17th century.

The staircase and half-landing through an arch of the Inner Hall, and below, a photograph c. 1929, showing the original staircase after Rateau's alterations. Before this the Inner Hall was a small drawing room. In the stairwell hang portraits of Lady Baillie's parents, 1st Lord Queenborough and Mrs Almeric Paget (who died before her husband became a peer).

This late 12th or early 13th century North Italian marble lion may have come from Venice. Holding a young ram between its paws, it originally supported a column of a portico.

53

Yellow Drawing Room

The Punchinello's Kitchen (detail) by Giambattista Tiepolo the elder.

Cylindrical Chinese vase, 18th century.

Mother-of-pearl bowl, ewer and dish, Eastern Mediterranean c.1650.

STRANGE MASKED MEN

in tall, pointed hats dominate this room. *The Punchinello's Kitchen* by Giambattista Tiepolo the elder (1696-1770), illustrates a moment's relaxation within the revels of Venetian Carnival. This Venetian artist was among the most brilliant of his generation, perhaps best known for his frescoes. His sumptuous and colourful paintings extended across classical, decorative, humorous and religious subjects. Above the ebonised and brass-edged William IV bookcases is a pair of flower pictures by Jean Baptiste Monnoyer (1634-99), a celebrated floral artist who worked for Louis XIV at Versailles, settling in England under the patronage of the Duke of Montagu *c*.1690. A library for most of the 19th century, the room's decorative scheme was created in 1938 by Boudin, who designed the *lambrequins* below the cornice and across the windows, one of his favourite ideas. It was not until after the end of World War II in 1945 that the room became a drawing room. The handsome Palladian chimneypiece is thought to have been brought to Leeds by 7th Lord Fairfax from the grand tour *c*.1730.

Among the many fine pieces of porcelain are the Chinese ruby coloured *famille rose* vases *c*.1736-95. The furniture is chiefly English, dating from late-17th and early-18th centuries.

Detail from the left hand flower painting by Jean Baptiste Monnoyer. The Leeds Castle paintings are among Monnoyer's most lavish, with three tiers of flowers garlanding and overflowing urns.

THORPE HALL ROOM

THE CARVED PINE PANELLING

and the superb Italian marble chimneypiece (probably carved by Edward Marshall, Master-Mason to the Crown) came from Thorpe Hall near Peterborough. This was designed for Chief Justice Oliver St. John by Peter Mills in 1653. Mills, with Sir Christopher Wren, was one of the architects who supervised the rebuilding of London after the Great Fire of 1666, having built the central block of Cobham Hall 1661-63. The panelling may have been worked by Thomas Whiting and Richard Cleere, and was installed in 1927, when it was stripped of its old green paint.

18th century Qianlong famille rose phoenix

19th century Chinese biscuit-ware ducks

There are good examples of English and French furniture dating mainly from the 18th century. Notable are nine George II walnut balloon-backed chairs c.1740, a pair of Louis XV beech armchairs c.1735 and a Queen Anne walnut armchair with unusual scrolled wings c.1710. The four striking gilt bronze wall lights are decorated with wyverns c.1750. The twelve-fold painted Chinese screen dates from the late 17th century Kangxi period. As in many other rooms, birds feature prominently, and there are several interesting examples of Chinese 18th and early-19th century porcelain and biscuit-ware.

French Empire clock c. 1805

18th century Chinese vase with ormolu handles now used as a lamp

Carved pine scroll

Chinese ridge tile rabbit

INNER AND FRONT HALLS

THE LUMLEY HORSEMAN

now presides over the inner hall. This important figure, in painted oak, is the earliest known equestrian statue in the history of English sculpture. Commissioned for Lumley Castle, Co. Durham, by the 7th Lord Lumley (1533-1609), one of the great collectors of his day, his inventory of 1590 states that it was made "*in memorie of King Edward the 3*". The sculptor's identity is not known, although he may have been a Flemish carver working in England.

In the front hall is a mid-17th century walnut and oak refectory table, and above it hangs a late-16th century Flemish verdure tapestry, woven with birds, flowers and large leaves. On the walls are three medieval great swords, dating from the 14th and early-15th centuries, and a German sword *c.*1500.

Detail from one of the two Flemish verdure tapestries, showing a lioness pursuing a lion among flowers, foliage and exotic birds, both probably woven at Grammont in the second half of the 16th century.

Refectory table and Flemish tapestry seen through front door.

OPPOSITE:
THE LUMLEY
HORSEMAN SEEN
FROM THORPE
HALL ROOM.

LIBRARY   DINING ROOM

Private Rooms

These rooms are used for conferences, meetings, receptions, dinners and banquets. With the exception of the bedrooms, they are incorporated into the visitor route whenever possible.

BOARDROOM   CASTLE BEDROOMS

English walnut and parcel gilt
bureau c. 1730

One of a pair of terrestrial
and celestial globes,
early 19th century

Detail of pelmet

Boy with a falcon, circle of
Wybrand Simonszoon de Geest,
16th century

LIBRARY

Twelve-sided Indian marble
table, the top inlaid with
birds and flowers

Since the New Castle's construction in 1822, this room has had several uses. Until 1926 it served as a small dining room. Lady Baillie used it first as a schoolroom where her daughters received their early education. In 1938 Stéphane Boudin redesigned it after a late-17th century model by Daniel Marot (1663-1752), who was probably the main architect working for the 1st Duke of Montagu at Boughton House, Northamptonshire. Marot was a French Huguenot refugee, who fled to the Court of William of Orange in 1684. On the shelves are books from Lady Baillie's collection, and also from the library of her father, Lord Queenborough, and above these are Chinese and Japanese 18th Century vases and other ornaments.

Italian bronze-mounted marble late-18th century vase.

FRENCH AND ENGLISH STYLES

of furniture and decoration were cleverly blended by Stéphane Boudin when he designed this room in 1938. Five late-18th century Louis XVI Aubusson pastoral tapestries are set in panels, and, at each end of the room and above the doors, pieces from Lady Baillie's collection of 18th century Chinese porcelain are displayed.

The William IV mahogany dining table contrasts with the white painted Louis XIV-style chairs and pier tables. Above the chimneypiece hangs a Louis XIV ormolu mounted clock attributed to the famous André-Charles Boulle, dating from the early-18th century. Boudin designed the ivory floral medallion carpet, which he later also supplied to the White House for Mrs Kennedy.

DINING ROOM

The five pedestal dining table can accommodate thirty diners when it is fully extended with intervening leaves.

The Boardroom conference table can seat up to twenty delegates.

The fireplace is decorated with Henry VIII's coat of arms and Tudor rose badge.

BOARDROOM

This room was rebuilt 1822-23, following the destruction of much of the Gloriette by French and Dutch prisoners of war held at Leeds Castle in the 1660s. The fireplace, with Tudor heraldry in its spandrels, was moved here from elsewhere in the castle by Rateau.

The linenfold panelling at the west end was installed by Rateau in 1927-29. Meetings of up to twenty people can be held around the Regency mahogany dining table, and against the walls are several interesting 17th century oak side tables. The red ministerial boxes were used by Lord Geoffrey-Lloyd, first Chairman of the Leeds Castle Foundation, when he was a member of Churchill's wartime administration.

Over the fireplace is a portrait of Anthony Collins (1676-1729),the father of Martha Collins, first wife of the Hon. Robert (later 7th Lord) Fairfax, of Leeds Castle (whose portraits hang in the Heraldry Room), attributed to Jonathan Richardson.

The Turret Bedroom, like many of the rooms, was beautifully decorated and furnished by Boudin. It contains interesting works of art such as the portrait of a midshipman attributed to Mason Chamberlain c.1780.

CASTLE BEDROOMS

TWENTY-ONE LUXURIOUS BEDROOMS

are available to those attending conferences and functions at Leeds Castle. There are three in the Gloriette and eighteen in the New Castle.

Green Bedroom: Dutch school portrait of child c.1620.

Trompe l'oeil painted chest of drawers supplied by Boudin in the Cream Bedroom.

The Cream Bedroom contains panelling installed in 1822.

Opposite: The Walnut Bedroom, showing three Dutch portraits of children, the central painting being Dordrecht school c.1620, flanked by two paintings by Anthonie Palamedesz, 1655.

Maiden's Tower

IN FRONT OF THE CASTLE IS A LARGE CIRCULAR LAWN, where croquet is played on occasions. As one looks at the front of the castle, to its right is the Maiden's Tower, which was reconstructed in the 16th century. The Wykeham Martins gave it its name in the 19th century, following the discovery that Christiana Hyde, a recluse, was allowed to live on this site during Richard II's reign. The crenellations were probably added by the Smythes when they rebuilt the New Castle in the early 17th century. Lady Baillie converted it back to domestic use in the late 1920s after years as a brewhouse and estate workshop. Until 2001 it was the home of Lady Baillie's late daughter, Susan (Mrs Edward Remington-Hobbs), and is now undergoing restoration in order to be incorporated within the visitor route and conference facilities. At the south end of the island is the Gatehouse, which contains rooms for entertaining and houses the Dog Collar Museum and shop.

The Maiden's Tower.

Lady Baillie at
Leeds Castle
with her
German
shepherd dog,
Elsa.

Portrait possibly of
Mr Francis Brand,
Gentleman of the Privy
Chamber, with a buck
hound. The dog's
collars are inscribed
'Hampton Court'
and '1671'.

DOG COLLAR MUSEUM

A UNIQUE COLLECTION

of historic and fascinating dog collars has been built up over the years
and is now the only one of its kind in Great Britain.

Dogs have always been present at Leeds Castle:
hounds for hunting, gundogs, huge mastiffs to guard the
gates, and lap dogs to grace the apartments of widowed
queens. Lady Baillie herself always had several dogs and
it is therefore fitting that Leeds Castle should be home to
this unique museum housed in the Gatehouse.

Most of the collars were generously presented to the Leeds Castle
Foundation by Mrs John Hunt in memory of her husband, a
distinguished Irish scholar. The collection, which spans 400 years, is
supplemented from time to time.

On the walls hang portraits of members of the Lumley family, painted
before 1590 for John, 7th Lord Lumley, and attributed to Sir William
Segar, Garter King of Arms.

In Lady Baillie's time the museum was
used as a squash court, having
previously been a coach house.

A French bronze
collar of 1800.

A German hinged
collar of the early-
1700s.

'Tabinet's' collar –
Lord Talbot's
winner of the
Great Champion
Puppy Stakes for
All England, 1838.

An Austrian collar
with the arms of
its owner of the
mid-1700s.

An Italian brass
collar of the mid-
1600s.

Detail of German portrait of
dogs belonging to an English
officer, late-18th century.

The LEEDS CASTLE story

ESLEDES

OVER ONE THOUSAND YEARS

ago the Saxons called it *Esledes,* and in time 'Leeds' grew
out of that original name. The manor of Leeds was a
possession of the Saxon royal family probably as early as the
reign of **Ethelbert IV** (856-860). In the years immediately
before the Conquest, King Edward the Confessor had
granted the manor to the powerful house of **Godwin**.

In 1090 William II *Rufus* granted the manor to a cousin,
Hamo de Crèvecoeur, who had come over with his father.
In 1119 **Robert de Crèvecoeur** began building the first
stone castle. The keep, or main fortification, was built on the
site of the present Gloriette. It is possible that without the
existence of the fortified mill, situated here on the River Len,
the castle would not have been built where it is. Although
impossible to date definitely, it is certain that the mill predates
the Domesday survey of 1086.

CRÈVECOEUR

Domestic buildings were located in the bailey on the larger
island, which was connected to the keep by a drawbridge over
a water-filled ditch. After the battle of Evesham in 1265, the
family fortunes went into decline and Sir Robert de Crèvecoeur
was obliged to yield the castle to Sir Roger de Leyburn whose
son William, 1st Lord Leyburn, conveyed the castle to **Edward
I** and his queen, **Eleanor of Castile** in 1278.

*Above and below: Watercolour of the mill ruins, and an
accurate plan of the intricate defensive waterworks of the
Barbican, by Thomas Charles, 1798.*

Courtesy of The Curator, Maidstone Museum and Art Gallery.

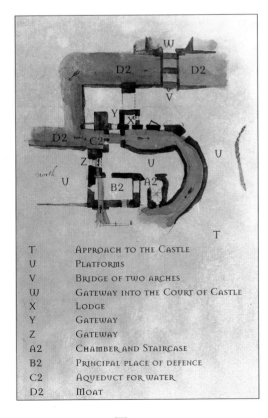

T	APPROACH TO THE CASTLE
U	PLATFORMS
V	BRIDGE OF TWO ARCHES
W	GATEWAY INTO THE COURT OF CASTLE
X	LODGE
Y	GATEWAY
Z	GATEWAY
A2	CHAMBER AND STAIRCASE
B2	PRINCIPAL PLACE OF DEFENCE
C2	AQUEDUCT FOR WATER
D2	MOAT

*The barbican at Leeds is of a unique
construction, being placed on the outer wall of
the dam, at this point reduced to 50 feet in
width. At the south end of the barbican was a
strongly fortified mill, ruined since the 1650s,
through which an aqueduct, in its basement
storey, conveyed water to flood the Len valley
when danger threatened.*

LEEDS

REST AND PLEASURE

So began the long royal ownership of Leeds Castle. Both Edward I and his queen, Eleanor, daughter of St. Ferdinand III, King of Castile, enjoyed Leeds and used it for resting and hunting. Queen Eleanor introduced refinements from her southern homeland, much influenced by the Moors, such as carpets for floors and walls and glass for windows. In medieval times marriage was regarded by kings almost entirely as a means of increasing or safeguarding power. It was to protect the southern boundary of his French possessions in Gascony that Edward originally married Eleanor.

Edward I
Courtesy of Mary Evans Picture Library

Eleanor of Castile

Courtesy of HULTON GETTY

The tomb of Eleanor of Castile in Westminster Abbey, London.
Courtesy of The Bridgeman Art Library

Between Harby, near Lincoln, where the queen died, and Charing Cross in London, the king erected 12 crosses as memorials where the royal bier rested. Of the three surviving Eleanor crosses, the triangular one at Geddington, Northamptonshire (left), is the best preserved. Built in 1294 it shows three recessed figures of the queen, and her and Edward I's coats of arms.

The arms of Eleanor of Castile are still flown above Leeds Castle on days commemorating her and her ownership.

The marriage may have been concluded for reasons of state but, like his parents Henry III and Eleanor of Provence, King Edward and Queen Eleanor grew to love each other. Edward I carried out extensive alterations to the castle and part of what is seen today stems from the work of the king's engineers. Taking advantage of the site, the embankments surrounding the moat were perfected. A large dam was constructed to hold in the waters, protected by a barbican of unusual design connected with the fortified mill and gatehouse. A revetment wall, some 30 feet high, rising sheer from the water, was built around the largest island, strengthened at intervals by semi-circular turrets which originally had loopholed upper storeys and contained garderobes. Domestic buildings occupied much of the main island, which drawbridges connected to the keep, here called the Gloriette (a Spanish term for a pavilion at the intersection of a Moorish garden, arising from Eleanor of Castile's influence). Queen Eleanor died in 1290 and in 1293 the king established a chantry in the castle to his beloved queen's memory. The chantry was confirmed and extended by succeeding monarchs down to its dissolution at the Reformation in 1544. In 1299, in order to improve relations with France, Edward I married Margaret, sister of Phillip III *le Hardi*, King of France, and they spent their honeymoon at Leeds Castle. The king granted Leeds to his queen, inaugurating the pattern whereby the castle often became part of the dower of the Queens of England and was retained by them during their widowhood. Things went less smoothly for **Edward II** and his

The gatehouse, from the site of the barbican, showing the gatetower brought forward by Edward I to strengthen the defences of the castle c.1280. Grooves for the portcullis, and a recess for the drawbridge and slits for its chains still exist. In the 1380s machicolations were added at parapet level to provide holes through which missiles and hot liquids could be dropped.

queen, **Isabella**, daughter of Philip IV *le Bel*, King of France. Neglecting to inform his wife, he granted the castle to **Bartholomew, Ist Lord Badlesmere** Lord Steward of the Household. One day in 1321, the queen arrived at the castle to seek rest and shelter, but was refused admission and was greeted by archers firing on the royal party, several of whom were killed. Not pleased with this response, the king besieged the castle and once he had captured him, had Badlesmere beheaded. Six years later Edward II was deposed and murdered, but Queen Isabella retained the castle until her death in 1358. Where the previous two Edwards had stopped, the next king, **Edward III**, continued their work and extended the park and greatly improved the castle.

HUMILIATION

Richard II adhered to tradition and granted Leeds Castle to his queen, **Anne of Bohemia** in 1382. After her untimely death in 1394, his love of Leeds Castle brought him back several times to conduct state business. In 1395 the castle was visited by the celebrated historian Froissart, who described Leeds as 'a beautiful Palace in Kent'.

This portrait of Richard II is to be seen in the Henry VIII Banqueting Hall. It is a 16th century copy of the famous contemporary portrait of the king in Westminster Abbey, one of the earliest examples of portraiture executed from life.

Like Edward II, Richard II was deposed. When he was secretly returned to Leeds disguised as a poor forester, awaiting his removal to Yorkshire, his days as King had ended. Leeds Castle saw Richard in his days of power, and in his days of humiliation.

Drama and intrigue were never far away from Leeds Castle. Henry IV's second queen, **Joan of Navarre** was granted the castle in 1403 and 11 years later granted it to the **Archbishop of Canterbury, Thomas Arundel**. Lord Cobham, the Lollard leader, was summoned to Leeds by the Archbishop to stand trial for heresy and was found guilty and beheaded. It is at this time that we first learn from the Archbishop's inventory the uses of the rooms in the Gloriette.

DIPLOMATIC CONVERSATIONS

In 1416 the holy Roman emperor Sigismund, the most powerful sovereign in Europe and brother of Anne of Bohemia (Richard II's queen), came to England on a state visit to Henry V and lodged at Leeds for a month. The stay seriously depleted the revenues of the kingdom. Unfortunately nothing came of the defensive and offensive alliance negotiated by the two sovereigns. This visit was the second occasion Leeds was used as the base for diplomatic conversations. The first had occurred in 1289 when Edward I returned from an extended visit to Gascony. Awaiting the king on his arrival in August was Anthony Bek, prince bishop of Durham. One of the king's closest advisers, he was the chief negotiator with the Keepers of Scotland to arrange the marriage of the king's heir, Prince Edward, and Margaret, the *Maid of Norway*, grand-daughter of Alexander III whom she had succeeded in 1286 as Queen of Scots. Bek's negotiations were successful although the Maid was aged only seven and the king's son was five. They counted for little, however, since optimism vanished when the *Maid of Norway* died on the voyage to Scotland in September 1290. Her death destroyed all Edward I's plans and led ultimately to the long and bitter wars between England and Scotland. The conversations at Leeds might have changed the course of English and Scottish history.

WITCHCRAFT

Queen Joan's stepson was **Henry V**. He initially treated her cordially, but in time he began to suspect the unpopular queen and her foreign courtiers of plots against him, and swiftly relations deteriorated. She was suddenly charged with plotting the king's death by witchcraft by the 'most high and horrible means'. Due to the confessor who had informed against her being strangled, we will never know the gruesome plans, and rather than being put to death she was imprisoned at Leeds Castle. Shortly before his death the king released Queen Joan and restored all her property to her, after which she lived peacefully and prosperously for many years. Her housekeeping accounts for her stay at Leeds in 1422 are in the castle's archives. A generation later during **Henry VI's** reign, witchcraft loomed large again at Leeds. Eleanor Cobham, Duchess of Gloucester and the king's aunt, was also similarly accused and imprisoned in the Castle and eventually condemned as a witch.

The castle bell and clock were installed in 1435 during the time of Catherine de Valois. One of the oldest in the country, the clock strikes the hours, and can be heard by visitors passing beneath the bell tower at the north end of the upper bridge corridor. It was rung specially when HM The Queen visited Leeds in 1981.

REMARKABLE DYNASTY

Queen Catherine and Owen Tudor had secretly married, and their son, Edmund, Earl of Richmond, later became the father of Henry VII. Thus they provided England with the remarkable dynasty whose most famous member perhaps was **Henry VIII**. Although he

HENRY VIII

only used Leeds as a staging post en route to meetings in France, Henry VIII was responsible for restoring the Gloriette and beautifying its royal apartments for his first queen, Catherine of Aragon. Drawing on large sums of money, he transformed Leeds into a magnificent castle to rival the beauty of French castles. By 1552, having lost most of its possessions in France, the crown had no further need of Leeds. Edward VI's Protectors therefore granted it to Sir Anthony St. Leger, of Ulcombe near Leeds, who had pursued a conciliatory policy for Henry VIII when Lord Deputy of Ireland.

EL-DORADO

Sir Anthony's great-grandson, **Sir Warham,** could not have been as wise as his ancestor. As a financial backer of Sir Walter Raleigh's ill-fated expedition to discover the legendary gold of El-Dorado, he was ruined when the project ended in disaster and he was forced to sell the castle to his wife's uncle, **Sir Richard Smythe**, in 1618. The Smythe family held lucrative

The Jacobean house built by the Smythe family, by an unknown artist c.1750, showing its square headed windows and prominent lead spouts and pipes, and the bell tower terminating with a cupola.

crown appointments, Sir Richard's father Thomas controlling the customs of London, while Sir Richard was receiver for the Duchy of Cornwall. Although the Smythes did not own Leeds for long, they were responsible for the development of the architecture of the castle when they rebuilt the principal buildings at the north end of the main island. The footings of their fine Jacobean house were re-discovered during repair work in the present house in 1993. Passing through the female line, the castle was then sold in 1632 to a St Leger connection, **Sir Thomas Culpeper**.

A BROKEN MAN

Some years later, during the Civil War, the castle was used by Parliament as one of its arsenals in Kent. Due to this, and his son **Sir Cheney Culpeper's** political inclinations, the castle was not ruined, unlike the castles of Corfe in Dorset and nearby Rochester in Kent. Sir Cheney was bankrupted at the Restoration in 1660, however, and when he died intestate three years later, he was a broken man.

5 MILLION ACRES

Now America enters the story of Leeds Castle, a connection which remains to this day. Sir Cheney's second cousin **Thomas, 2nd Lord Culpeper** (*left*) used the dowry of his wealthy wife, **Margaret van Hesse** (*left*), to purchase Leeds Castle from the creditors of Sir Cheney's estate in 1663.

1660

His father John, 1st Lord Culpeper, an astute and loyal servant of King Charles I, had been instrumental in conveying the young Prince of Wales out of England and into exile in France, and had been rewarded for his loyalty by the grant of more than five million acres of land in Virginia. The yearly rental for this land between the Potomac and Rappahanock rivers was £6.13s. 4d.

UNWILLING GUESTS

During the mid-1660s Lord Culpeper leased the castle to the government as a place of detention for French and Dutch prisoners of war. Lodged in the Gloriette, the prisoners on one occasion set fire to their accommodation, causing damage which remained unrepaired until 1822. In 1676, following the failure of Nathaniel Bacon's rebellion in Virginia, the brother of the queen of a Native American tribe was sent to England as a hostage and was kept at Leeds Castle. Named 'William', he died here in 1678 and was buried at Broomfield church nearby.

A drawing of 1773 clearly showing the damage sustained to the Gloriette by the prisoners' arson.

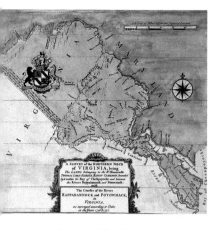

In 1680 Lord Culpeper took leave of Leeds Castle and was appointed Governor of Virginia. By his daughter **Catherine's** marriage to **Thomas, 5th Lord Fairfax** in 1690, and on her death in 1719, the castle passed to the Fairfax family.

America

During the ensuing 50 years the Fairfax ownership of the Virginia estate was continually challenged by the Colonial government and settlers. It was not until 1745 that the **6th Lord Fairfax** finally achieved confirmation of the family's sole rights, and sailed for Virginia to settle there for life, leaving the castle to his brother Robert. In doing so he became the only peer known to have settled permanently in America in colonial times. When he arrived in Virginia, lodging initially with his cousin William at Belvoir, near present day Alexandria, he struck up a friendship with the 16 year old George Washington, later to become the first president of the United States of America. Although the War of Independence was to separate the two families politically, General Washington retained his affection and friendship for the Fairfax family and Thomas in particular.

Thomas 6th Lord Fairfax
Masonic Temple, Alexandria, Virginia.

The time at the Fairfax seat in Virginia is indicated five hours behind Leeds on this sundial of 1750, to be seen outside the New Castle. In America there was a sundial giving the time at Leeds.

Wealthy wives

His brother **Robert Fairfax** was to own Leeds Castle for 46 years, and in that time undertook a large scale programme of improvements facilitated by the wealth of his two wives; Martha Collins, a banking heiress, and Dorothy Best. The exterior of the Smythe house was embellished with fashionable 'Strawberry Hill Gothik' features to the windows and door surrounds. Before the visit by King George III and Queen Charlotte following a review of the army at Coxheath in 1778, he spent large sums on refurbishing the drawing rooms for his royal guests' use. On his death in 1793 the property passed to his nephew the **Revd Dr Denny Martin** and in 1800 to **General Philip Martin**, the doctor's brother. In 1806 the American Virginia properties were sold, realising £14,000, plus £25,000 in compensation, and on his death in 1821 the general's fortune was left to a distant kinsman **Fiennes Wykeham,** of Chacombe in Northamptonshire. Fiennes added the name of his benefactor to his own, and so became Wykeham Martin, a name that was to have a profound effect on the appearance of the castle we see today.

A century of ownership

William Baskett, an architect from Camberwell, was instructed to demolish the Smythe house and build one in the style of Henry VII. Starting work in May 1822, the roof was raised in September and in 1823 the New Castle, as it became known, was finished. The final result prompted the famous castle historian Lord Conway to

Two drawings by Fiennes Wykeham Martin's daughter, Eliza, showing the castle in 1821 before its restoration (above), and the final result in 1823 (here).

comment; 'It possesses one great merit...it enters perfectly into the general complex of the whole' – in other words, it all blended with the existing architecture very satisfactorily. New drives were also created and the main entrance to the castle was altered to join the Maidstone - Folkestone road where it does today. The total bill for the work amounted to £33,955.00, a sum approaching £3 million at today's prices. As a result Wykeham Martin experienced financial difficulties and was forced to sell the contents of the castle at auction. Fortunately the trustees of General Philip Martin's will were able to purchase the Leeds Abbey estate when the Calcrafts sold it in 1839 and this enabled Charles Wykeham Martin to rebuild the family's fortune. Charles's first wife was Lady Jemima Mann. His second, Matilda Trollope, was a cousin of Anthony Trollope. An occasional visitor to the castle, it is possible that the *Courcy Castle* in his *Barsetshire* novels is based on Leeds. When the Wykeham Martin family acquired the Duppa estate at Hollingbourne in 1895, Leeds became one of the largest estates in central Kent.

DEATH DUTIES

In 1924, one hundred years after the Wykeham Martin restoration and rebuilding, the family were forced to sell the property in anticipation of having to pay crippling death duties. One of the potential buyers was the American newspaper magnate, Randolph Hearst, the inspiration for Orson Welles's all-time classic film *Citizen Kane*. On receiving adverse reports about the castle, his interest waned and it was eventually acquired by the **Honourable Mrs Wilson Filmer**, who saw the potential for such a home, and had, as it turned out, the style, imagination and importantly the means, to carry this out.

Anglo-American by birth, Olive Paget was the eldest daughter of Almeric Paget Lord Queenborough, GBE, and his wife Pauline, (above), daughter of the Hon. William Whitney, United States Navy Secretary in President Cleveland's first administration. She married her third husband, Sir Adrian Baillie, Bt, in 1931(right).

LADY BAILLIE

Lady Baillie, as she became, set about the task with her characteristic vigour, completely restoring the fabric and structure of the castle. Having spent much of her early life in France, it was perhaps inevitable that she would turn to French designers and artists to create her vision of what the interior of the castle should be. Both Rateau and Boudin created the interior decoration we see today and the improvement of Leeds Castle became her life's work. She lived longer at Leeds than any other owner in history, and her work on and for the castle ranks with that of any previous owner down the centuries. It was not all hard work however, and during the 1930s Leeds Castle became one of the great houses of England and a centre of lavish hospitality for leading politicians, ambassadors, foreign royalty and film stars. During World War II the castle was secretly employed to develop weapons and safety systems, and the minister responsible for this, Geoffrey Lloyd, became the first Chairman of the Leeds Castle Foundation, which Lady Baillie worked so hard to establish towards the end of her life. Leeds Castle and its surrounding park were bequeathed to the **Leeds Castle Foundation** in 1974.

PARK AND GARDENS

Opposite: Wild whooper swans are winter visitors to this country from northern Europe and Russia, but at Leeds Castle they can be seen all year round.

PARK

THE CREATION OF LEEDS CASTLE

park dates from the early-Middle Ages. The park was designed to enhance the architecture and status of the royal castle at its core. The original moated prospect, approaches and parkland setting of the gloriette may be attributable to the late-13th century Norman and Spanish Islamic influences associated with Edward I and his wife, Eleanor of Castile. From that time until the reign of Henry VIII, state papers and manorial records reveal the continuous presence of kings and queens at Leeds, and a constant round of additions and repairs to the royal parkland and woods. Thomas Hogben's survey in 1748 is the earliest detailed plan of the estate, and reveals remnants of the medieval and Tudor parks, in addition to later features. Much of the replanting of trees undertaken after the great storm of October 1987 followed Hogben's survey. The park continues to provide a picturesque visual backdrop to the castle buildings today.

In 1748 this map was commissioned by Robert Fairfax (later 7th Lord), one year after he became owner of the castle. This detail shows how the castle and its surrounding moat has altered little since then, but the Great Water to the right of the causeway – not flooded at that time – now occupies the areas surrounded by blue: 'Pigeon house Brook' and 'Horse Pasture'.

Courtesy of the Centre for Kentish Studies, Kent County Council

The resident bird population of the Duckery and Park is swelled each winter by wild waterfowl such as diving ducks and more unusual species like the goosander.
Steve Knell - RSPB Images

One of the first attractions on entering the grounds is the Duckery (left), created in the 1960s for Lady Baillie by the international garden designer Russell Page. Out of a tangled morass of brambles and fallen trees, a haven for wildfowl was constructed, with further cosmetic work being carried out in 1990 to build banks and resting places. In addition to the collection of wildfowl at Leeds, both in the Duckery and around the moat, the beautiful surroundings play host to a great number of species of wild birds: great crested grebes, kingfishers, sparrowhawks, and green and great spotted woodpeckers. In the summer spotted flycatchers, swifts, house martins and wagtails nest around the castle.

The Park

*A beautiful
statue given
to Lady Baillie.*

*A willow tree
acts as a
beguiling curtain.*

*Black swan
and daffodils.*

*Bluebells cluster around the trunk of
a beech tree.*

*May heralds the season of cherry
blossom.*

WHATEVER THE SEASON,

a beautiful statue of a female figure presides over the Wood Garden, which was designed to be at its best in spring. At this time of the year the place bursts into colour and life as daffodils, anemones and narcissi push up by the ash, willow and alder trees in carpets of yellow, blue and white.

Both sides of the River Len have been improved and further planting has taken place to add colour at other seasons. Summer flowering perennials and shrubs have been added to the rhododendrons and azaleas in the Pavilion Garden, which used to contain two tennis courts and is overlooked by Lady Baillie's attractive rustic tennis pavilion. Leeds Castle golf course was laid out in the early 1930s to a design by Major Sir Guy Campbell. Well known as a golfing author and an International for Scotland in 1909,1910 and 1911, Campbell laid out several new courses including the 9-hole course at Tides Inn, Irvington on the Northern Neck of Virginia in 1944.

In all, the Castle is surrounded by some 500 acres of gardens and park, containing the golf course, and a small agricultural estate beyond these. Whatever the season there is much to see and enjoy.

*The spectacular
cedar trees in the
park were planted
during the 1840s.*

The Culpeper Garden is home to the national collection of bergamot registered with the National Council for the Conservation of Plants and Gardens.

Flower beds are arranged in an informal pattern with low box hedges as borders. This very English garden is characterised by roses, pinks, lupins, poppies and lad's love, but with exotic blooms mixed in to create a profusion of colour and scent.

CULPEPER GARDEN

FOR MANY GENERATIONS

this had been the castle's kitchen garden, then it became a cut-flower garden during Lady Baillie's ownership, until it was transformed in 1980 by Russell Page into a large cottage garden. It takes its name from the Culpeper family which owned the castle in the 17th century. The herb border along the old wall would please Nicholas Culpeper, the famous 17th century herbalist, and a distant relation of the Leeds branch of the family.

Female eclectus
parrot

Bali starling

Toco toucan

Male eclectus parrot

Female and male
von der Decken's
hornbills

AVIARY

LADY BAILLIE'S

Australian finches were housed in aviaries at Leeds,
first established in the1950s. She continued to add
many rare and varied species, particularly parakeets.
The collection today is comprised of over 100
species and the new aviary buildings, designed by
the architect Vernon Gibberd, and opened in 1988,
incorporate the most progressive ideas in aviculture.

The twin aims of the collection are to
foster public awareness of the
importance of wildlife conservation, and
equally to increase an already
successful breeding programme with a
view to re-introducing threatened
species back into their natural habitats.

Scarlet ibis

A more detailed book
on the birds of Leeds
Castle is on sale at
the castle's shops and
at the aviary
information point.

Crowned
crane

Maze and Grotto

Maze – to bewilder, to amaze, to perplex –

certainly true of the wonderful creation at Leeds Castle.
At the end of a winding route, a series of unexpected
delights awaits the visitor to the Grotto.

Planted in 1988 with
2,400 yew trees, the
maze leads to a
spiralling path up to a
raised viewpoint which
gives panoramic views
of the park. It has the
appearance of a topiary
castle, and perceptive
viewers will be able to
see that part of the

maze's plan mirrors a queen's crown. Labyrinths, or mazes, developed from an
ancient Egyptian building near Lake Maeris which contained twelve courts and
3,000 chambers. The maze is a remnant of the historical geometric style of
planting.

Designed by Vernon Gibberd in collaboration with Minotaur Designs, the sculptor
Simon Verity and the shell artist Diana Reynell, the Grotto presents the 'underworld'
in a series of macabre forms and representations: alchemy, fossils, bones and
mythical beasts created out of shells, minerals, wood and other materials. As
daylight and the tunnel exit approaches, the theme lightens with the idea of rebirth
in the form of a shell phoenix.

Visitors are sped on their way by the *Green Man* about to spring out of his cave
and open the gate with his key.

GROTTO

The giant Typhoeus, father of the Harpies, tried to overpower the gods but was vanquished by Zeus and placed under Mount Etna (Sicily), where he became the source of fire. Here Typhoeus struggles against the weight of the mountain, lava flowing from his mouth. The dome is decorated with black and white swans, symbols of alchemy and of Leeds Castle.

GREENHOUSES AND VINEYARD

THE TRADITION OF HORTICULTURE

at Leeds Castle goes back to the 1730s, when Lord Fairfax sent chinquapin, wild olive, ginseng and indigo roots from Virginia to the hothouses at the castle. In exchange, apple trees were sent from Kent to the Shenandoah Valley in Virginia, where the area is still famed for its apple growing.

Today the greenhouses provide peaches, nectarines and other produce for the castle table. Many of the colourful blooms from the greenhouses are displayed throughout the castle all year round.

The vineyard at Leeds may be situated on the same site as the one recorded in Domesday Book in 1086. The wine, made from a blend of Müller Thurgau and Seyval Blanc grapes, is sold in the restaurant and shops under its own label. Riechensteiner and Schönberger vines have been planted recently to widen the range of wine produced in the future.

Plants grown at Leeds Castle are on sale at the new plant centre near the ticket office.

The Castle Flower and Produce Festivals

Held during summer and autumn, these festivals fill the castle's magnificent interior with exotic flower displays and creative presentations of produce from the Garden of England.

LADY BAILLIE GARDEN

OPENED IN 1999

by HRH Princess Alexandra, Patron of the Leeds Castle Foundation,
the garden was designed by the landscape architect, Christopher Carter,
on the site of Lady Baillie's aviary.

Of contrasting character to the Culpeper Garden, the dramatic new
terraces, with their panoramic views across the Great Water, have
established themselves as an attraction in their own right. The folded
terrace wall encloses intimate suntraps, rich with Mediterranean and sub-
tropical plants, providing flowers throughout the year.

*Sculpted
commemorative sundial
featuring a toucan, one of
Lady Baillie's favourite species of bird.*

The Lady Baillie Garden
opened by
H.R.H Princess Alexandra
Patron of the
Leeds Castle Foundation
on the 21st May 1999

FOOD,

Fairfax Hall

A superbly restored 17th century barn serves as a licensed self-service restaurant seating up to 150 people. Available for private functions.

Terrace Room

With spectacular views of the castle, this oak-beamed extension to the Fairfax Hall offers an excellent menu with table service for up to 80 people. Available for private functions.

Fairfax Courtyard

Situated here are several outlets serving refreshments.

Wykeham Martin Tea Room

Built beside the greenhouses, this offers a selection of light refreshments.

DRINK

The Park Shop and Plant Centre

Situated at the main entrance, this is filled with an array of interesting and unusual souvenirs and gifts, which are based on a floral theme, as well as plenty for the animal lover and garden enthusiast. During November and December it becomes a wonderful Christmas shop, full of lovely presents and decorations. The Plant Centre features plants grown at Leeds Castle, many of which can be seen in the gardens.
No admission to the castle is necessary.

The Dog Collar Museum Shop

Situated within our unique Dog Collar Museum, this offers beautiful tapestries as well as a superb collection of canine-themed gifts.

The Courtyard Shop

This traditional gift shop offers quality souvenirs such as china and glass, tapestries and pictures, as well as chutneys and jams, and Leeds Castle's own wine.

S H O P P I N G

*Left:
Detail of painting in the Queen's
Gallery attributed to
Jan Janszoon de Heem, c.1700.*

ENTERTAINMENT

ENTERTAINMENT AND EVENTS

are as much a part of Leeds as the Castle
and the Grounds.

There cannot be a more perfect setting for a round of
golf, an open-air concert, a spectacular firework
display or children's events. Leeds Castle has
become famous for the Great Balloon and Vintage
Car Fiesta and performances by world famous stars
such as Luciano Pavarotti and Sir Elton John. Each
summer the renowned open air concerts are held,
under such celebrated conductors as Carl Davis with
famous orchestras like the Royal Liverpool
Philharmonic, together with notable soloists. Leeds
Castle plays host to a variety of special events and
entertainments which take place throughout the year.
These include the New Year's Day Treasure Trail, the
Festival of English Food and Wine, Half Term Fun for
Children, Flower Festivals and celebrations of
Christmas and Easter. The firework display held
annually on or near to November 5th is the largest
and most spectacular in the South of England.

Leeds Castle Public Golf Course is a challenging and
scenic 9-hole course which is open to all.
Redesigned by Neil Coles MBE, it is open all year
round.

Telephone numbers:

Golf Centre	01622 767828
Events/Concerts Box Office	01622 880008
Reception and Reservations Office	01622 765400

"The
LOVELIEST CASTLE
in the World"

THE OWNERS OF LEEDS CASTLE

Holders of the Manor of Leeds

856-860	Ethelbert IV (under King of Kent), King of England 860-866
1052-53	Earl Godwin
1053-66	Earl Lewin
1066	William I *The Conqueror*
1066-90	Odo, Earl of Kent, Bishop of Bayeaux
1090	William II Rufus
1090-1119	Hamo de Crèvecoeur
	Etard de Crèvecoeur

Holders of Leeds Castle and the Manor of Leeds

	Robert de Crèvecoeur
	Daniel de Crèvecoeur
	Hamo de Crèvecoeur
d.1263	Hamo de Crèvecoeur
1263-68	Sir Robert de Crèvecoeur, KB
1268-71	Sir Roger de Leyburn
1271-78	William, 1st Lord Leyburn
1278-90	Queen Eleanor (of Castile)
1290-1297	Edward I
1297-99	Isabella, Lady de Vesci
1299-1317	Queen Margaret (of France)
1317-21	Bartholomew, 1st Lord Badlesmere
1321-27	Edward II
1327-58	Queen Isabella (of France)
1358-77	Edward III
1377-82	Richard II
1382-94	Queen Anne (of Bohemia)
1394-99	Joan, Lady de Mohun
1399	Henry IV
1399-1403	Sir John Norbury
1403-12	Queen Joan (of Navarre)
1412-14	Thomas Arundel, Archbishop of Canterbury
1414-19	Joan, Countess of Hereford
1419-22	Henry V
1422-37	Queen Catherine (de Valois)
1437-49	Sir John Steward, KB
1449-61	Henry VI
1461-83	Edward IV
1483	Edward V
1483-85	Richard III
1485-1509	Henry VII
1509-47	Henry VIII
1547-52	Edward VI
1552-59	Sir Anthony St Leger, KG
1559-97	Sir Warham St Leger
1597-1602	Anthony St Leger Esq.
1602-18	Sir Warham St Leger
1618-28	Sir Richard Smythe
1628-32	Sir John Smythe
1632	Elizabeth, Lady Thornhill and Mary, Mrs Barrow
1632	Sir Thomas Culpeper, MP
1632-63	Sir Cheney Culpeper
1663-89	Thomas, 2nd Lord Culpeper
1689-1710	Margaret, Lady Culpeper
1710-19	Catherine, Lady Fairfax
1719-47	Thomas, 6th Lord Fairfax
1747-93	Hon. Robert Fairfax, MP, afterwards 7th Lord
1793-1800	Revd Dr Denny Martin, afterwards Fairfax
1800-21	General Philip Martin
1821-40	Fiennes Wykeham Martin Esq.
1840-70	Charles Wykeham Martin Esq. MP
1870-78	Philip Wykeham Martin Esq., MP
1878-93	Elizabeth, Mrs Wykeham Martin
1893-1924	Cornwallis Philip Wykeham Martin Esq.
1924-26	Fairfax Wykeham Martin Esq.
1926-74	Hon. Olive, Lady Baillie

Owners of Leeds Castle in Perpetuity

Leeds Castle Foundation from 1974

THE LEEDS CASTLE FOUNDATION

*The Leeds Castle Foundation coat of arms granted in 1999
to mark the 25th anniversary of the Foundation.*

The Foundation is a charity established by the Hon Olive, Lady Baillie with the priority of preserving the castle and its grounds in perpetuity for the benefit and enjoyment of the public. The charity also has wider duties including the use of the castle and grounds for cultural and artistic purposes and for funding significant national and international seminars, particularly those related to medical issues. Lady Baillie envisaged a living castle rather than a museum and anticipated that a wide range of activities would be needed to support the maintenance of the castle, its park and gardens and other amenities.

The Foundation has received no government funding. It is self-financing. The Trustees, both directly and through Leeds Castle Enterprises Ltd (a wholly owned subsidiary whose net income is covenanted to the Foundation), seek to balance the need to raise substantial funds to fulfil their fundamental responsibilities with protecting the unique character and quality of the castle as an historic house in a peaceful and beautiful setting.